I0089234

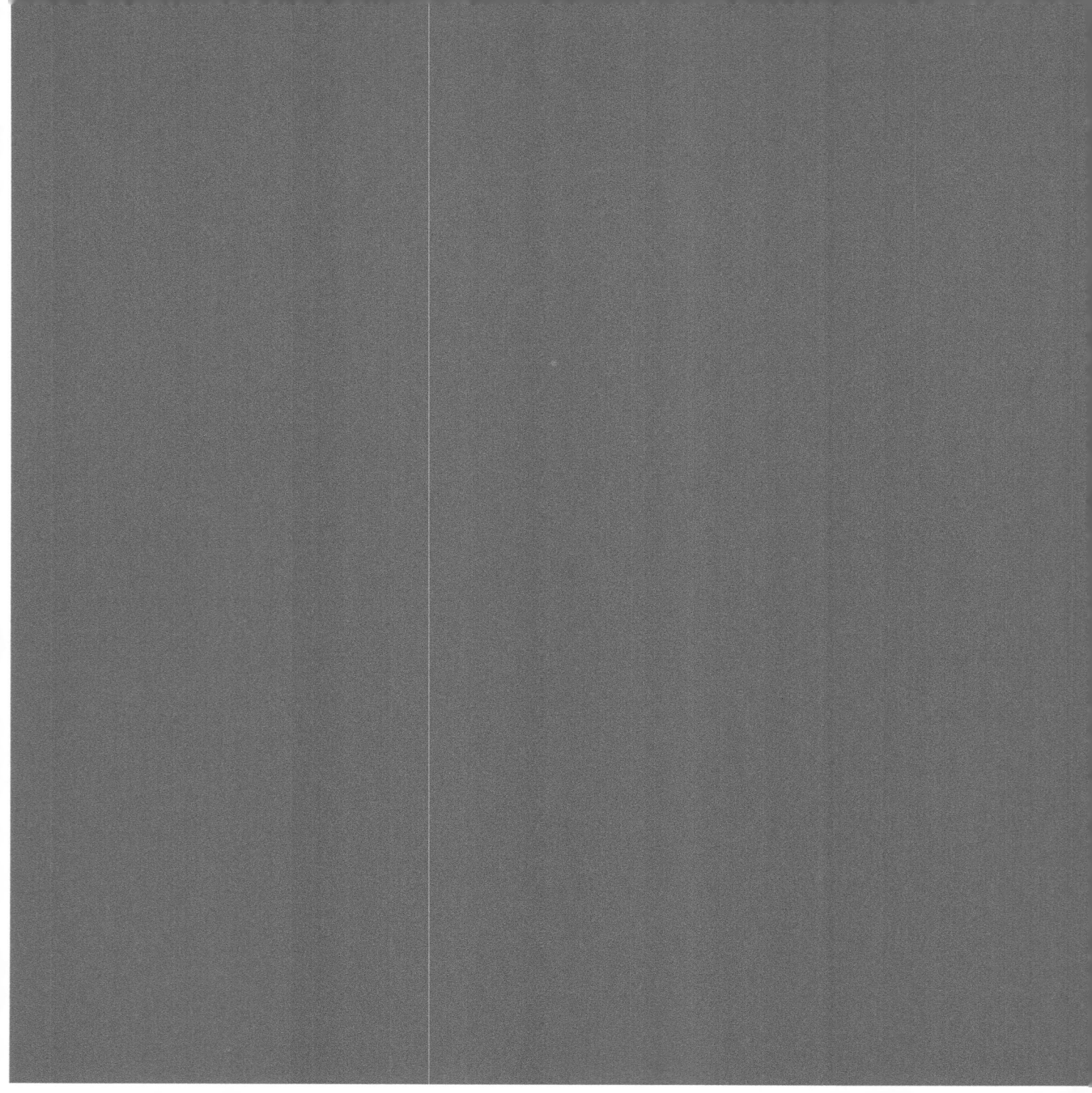

This book is dedicated to:

Steve Naples & Pat Gremo
Walt Frueh & Dallas Frueh

Thank you so much for helping me to understand minicup stock car racing (and for helping to convince my parents to let me get into the sport). My life is forever changed because of it.

ZACHARY TINKLE'S

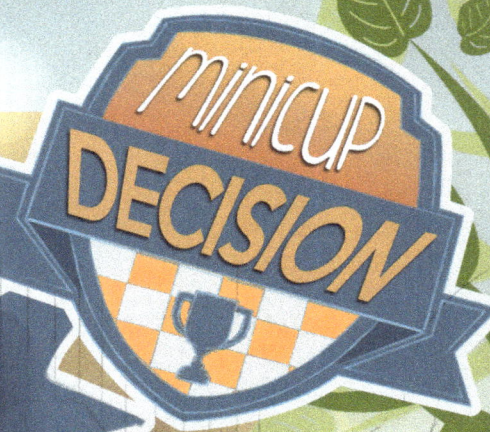

minicup
DECISION

58

Text and illustrations copyright © 2015 Zachary Tinkle /Left Paw Press

All rights reserved. No part of this book may be reproduced or transmitted in any form or by any means, electronic or mechanical, including photocopying, recording, or by an information storage retrieval system, without express written permission from the publisher.

No patent liability is assumed with respect to the use of information contained herein. Although every precaution has been taken in the preparation of this book, the publisher and author assume no responsibility for errors or omissions nor is any liability assumed for damages resulting from the use of the information contained herein.

All terms mentioned in this book that are known to be trademarks or service marks have been appropriately capitalized. Left Paw Press cannot attest to the accuracy of this information. Use of a term in this book should not be regarded as affecting the validity of any trademark or service mark.

Every effort has been made to make this book as complete and as accurate as possible, but no warranty or fitness is implied. The information provided is on an "as is" basis. The author and the publisher shall have neither liability nor responsibility to any person or entity with respect to any loss or damages arising from the information contained in this book.

Left Paw Press, publishing imprint of Lauren Originals, Inc.

ISBN: 978-1-943356-07-2

Library of Congress Control Number: 2015944048

PRINTED IN THE UNITED STATES OF AMERICA

Author: Zachary Tinkle

Illustrations: Antonio J. "Nunoh" Díaz

For educational, corporate, or retail sales accounts, email: info@laurenoriginals.com. For information, address: Left Paw Press, c/o Lauren Originals, Inc. 8926 N Greenwood Avenue #293 Niles, IL 60714. Left Paw Press can be found on the web at www.leftpawpress.com.

It was springtime. The sun was shining. Birds were chirping. And, I was PUMPED! Racing season was about to begin.

You see, I was getting ready take another step toward my dream of being a NASCAR® driver. I was going to start go-kart racing outdoors since I won an indoor go-kart championship the fall before. It was time for me to move up.

My coach thought I was ready too.

We'd been practicing for months.

One night, my parents saw that one of the most famous NASCAR® drivers was going to be in town signing autographs at a local car show. So, we went to the convention center early to get a good spot in line.

I did not want to miss my chance to meet this guy and see his big hat in person.

Well, on the way back to the very back of the convention center to get to the line, we saw a booth from a distance. It had in it one of the craziest things I'd ever seen. I could not believe my eyes.

In that booth, there were cars that looked like NASCAR® stock cars, but they were MY size. They were made for someone like ME. Can you believe it? It was the coolest thing I'd ever seen.

My dad wondered if they were toys. My mom wondered if they were cars that the Shriners® drove in the parades.

I just wanted to know if I could get into it and drive it.

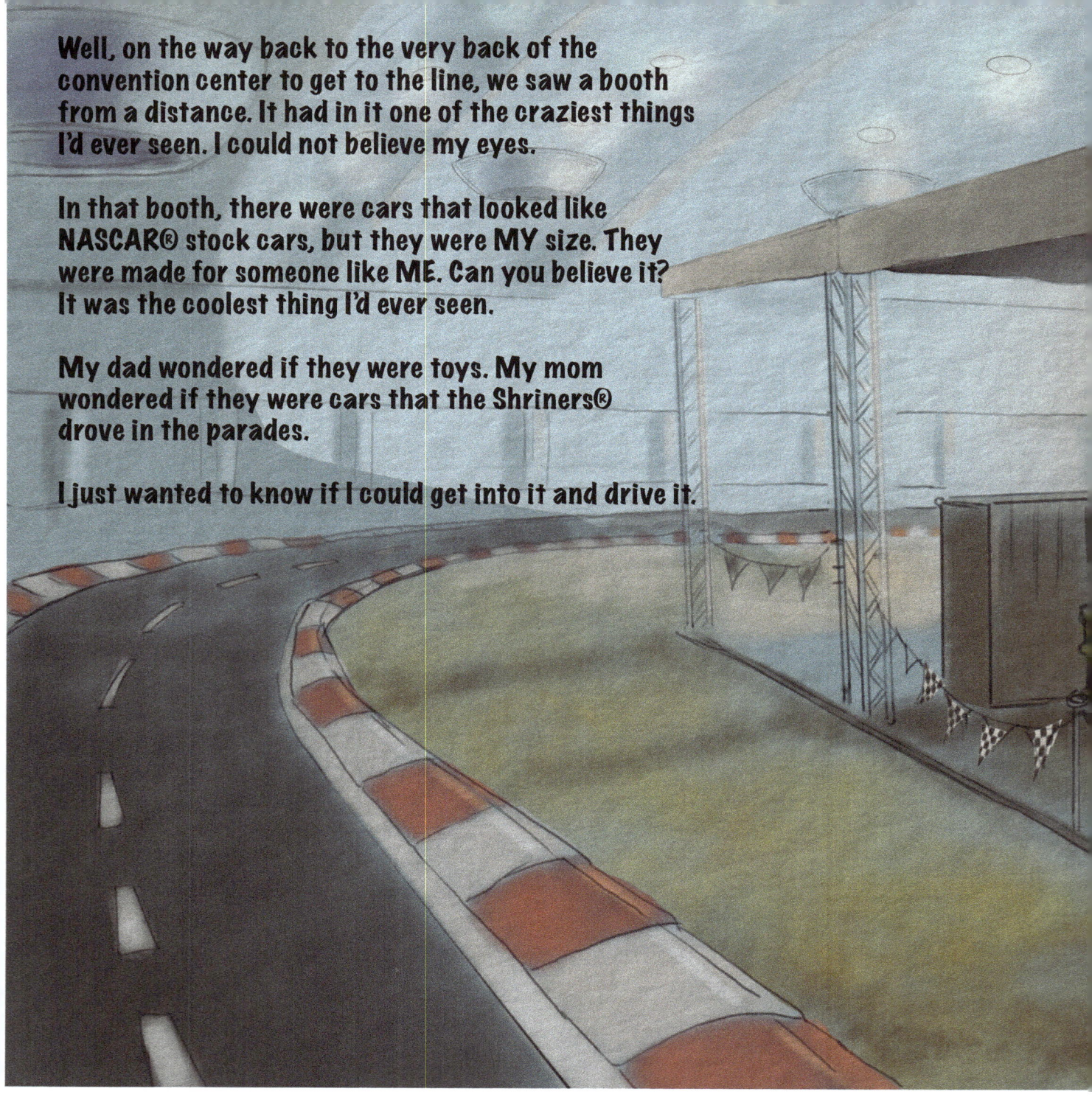

We stopped to talk to a man and his fiancée at the booth.

They explained that these were REAL racecars called minicups, which are ½ size stock cars.

These people actually raced these on local asphalt tracks.

I was shocked when they told me they could go over 100 miles per hour on a big enough track.

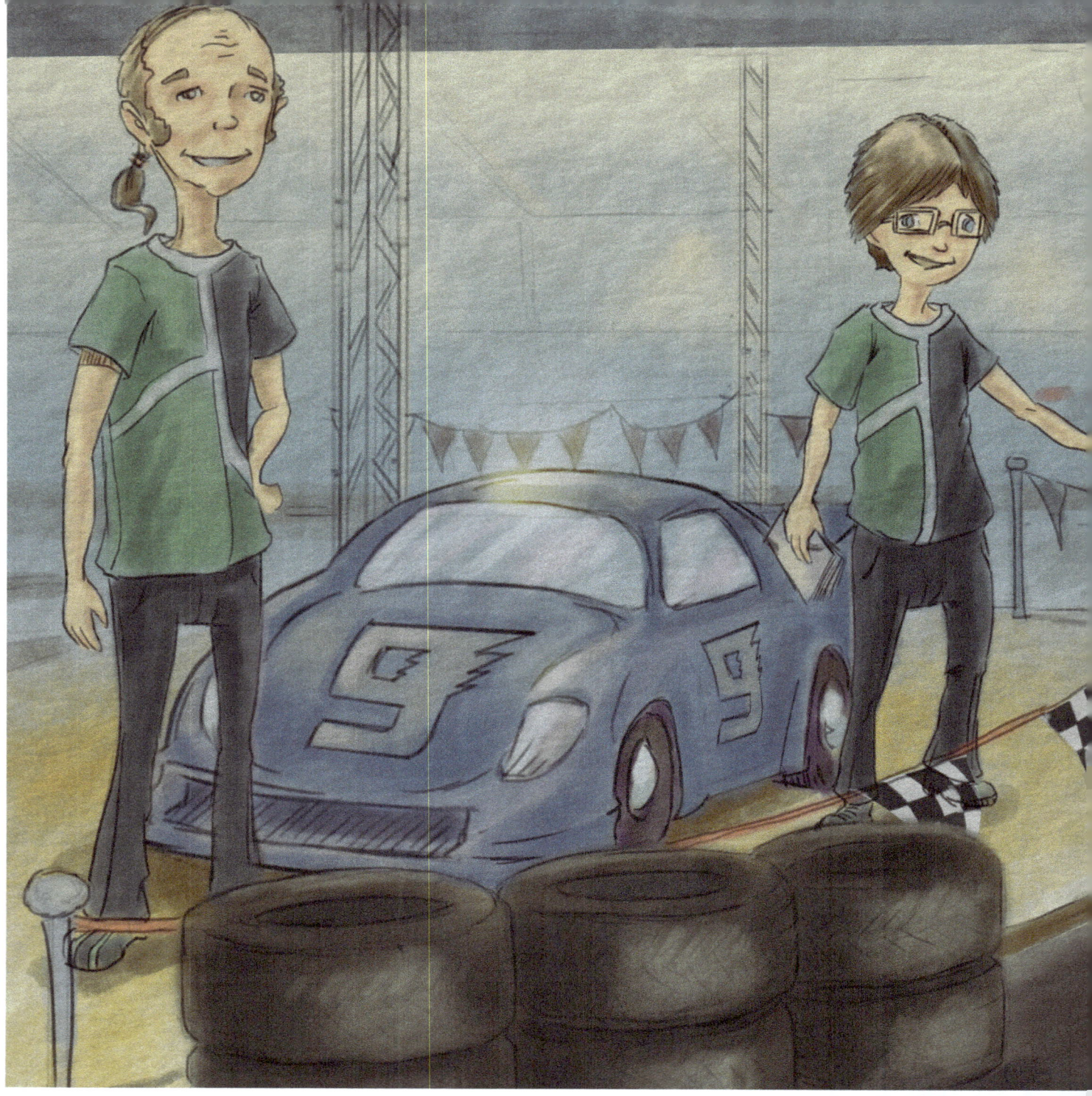

There was another man and his son in the booth.

Apparently they were a team. Dad was the mechanic and crew and the son was the driver. I liked this kid. When I asked him about racing, he was straight with me about the ups and downs. But, I could tell he was like me and loved being on a racetrack. He even gave me a signed hero card — just like the drivers at the speedways.

GARAGE MIRACLE

We went to get in line for the autographs, but I couldn't stop thinking about those minicup stock cars.

I went back three times to check them out again. You see, the problem with all this was the money we'd already spent on a go-kart and coaching.

I felt like I had already started down a path and there was no way out of it.

When I went home that night, I couldn't sleep.

I paced.

The next day, I couldn't stop thinking about those cars.

I paced some more.

My parents told me that I'd better say what was on my mind. I paced some more. Then, after a lot of thought, I got up the courage to make my case.

We sat down and I told my mom and dad that my dream was to be a NASCAR® driver someday. And, I thought that the minicup car would better prepare me for NASCAR®.

They have the same chassis and body. You have similar safety equipment like the seat, five-point harness, helmet, fireproof suit, radios and a spotter.

I went on and on and on like an attorney arguing in front of the Supreme Court.

When I was done, my parents didn't say anything. They just looked at each other. Then they grinned and chuckled.

Was the joke on me? What was going on?

They said that they had been privately talking and saying the same thing, but that this was a decision I had to own myself since it would affect my entire racing career.

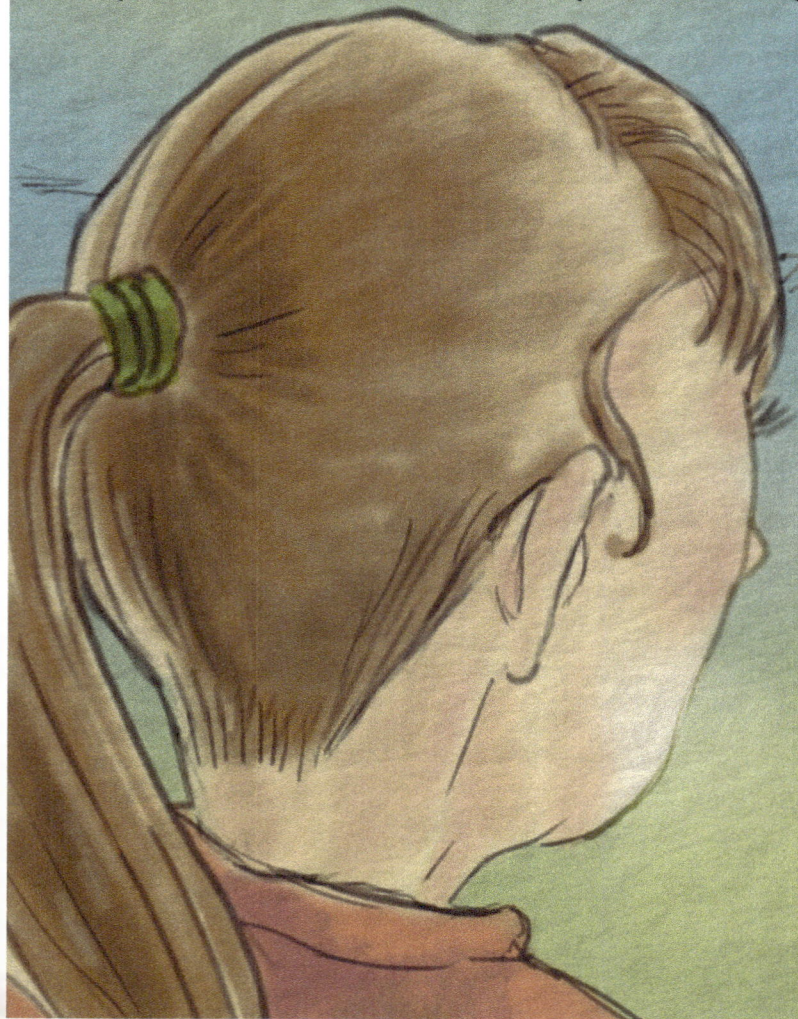

My mom called the number on the minicup club card and talked to the manager of the league about tracks, maintenance, safety, differences between go-karts and minicups, costs, the season, rules, and other stuff.

It was a long call, but she went ahead and scheduled a time to meet.

I felt like I could burst.

This was a decision of a lifetime and I knew with every part of me that this was the right one.

When the day came, it took over an hour to get to motorsports place where they had the minicups.

It felt like ten.

FINALLY, I could get in one.

I LOVED it.

We made a deal on the minicup that I knew was meant to be mine.

And, when we shook hands, the league manager made me promise that when I raced my first Daytona 500®, I'd get him a helicopter ride to the race.

Then he asked me what my goal was going to be for my first year. I didn't hesitate one bit. I told him, "I want to be Rookie of the Year."

But, that is another story for another day!

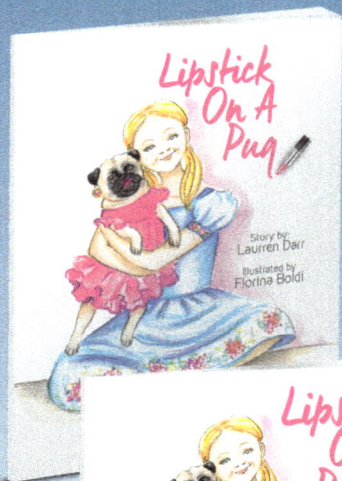

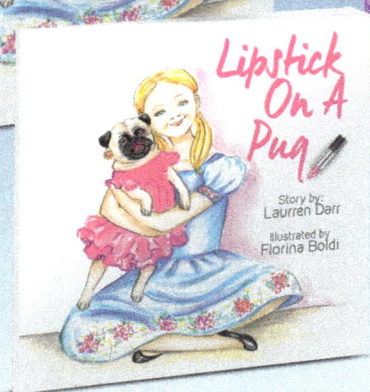

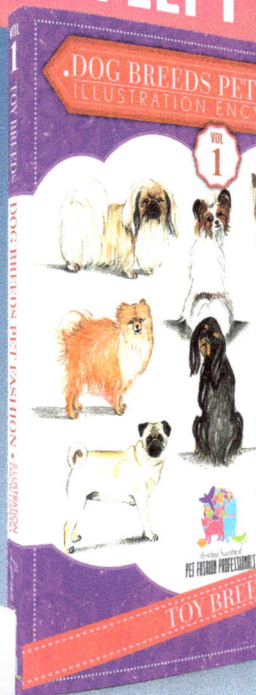

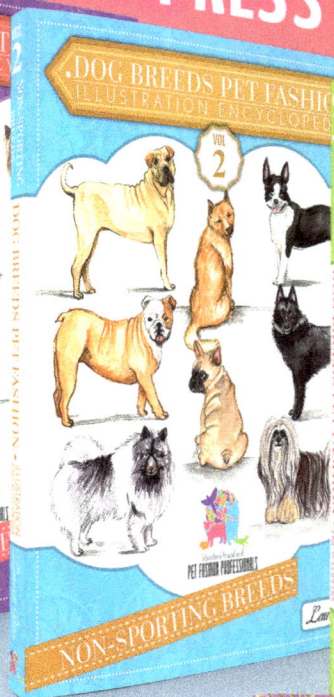

❦LEFT PAW Press !

PROUDLY PUBLISHES MEDICAL BOOKS BY
DR. BRAD T TINKLE

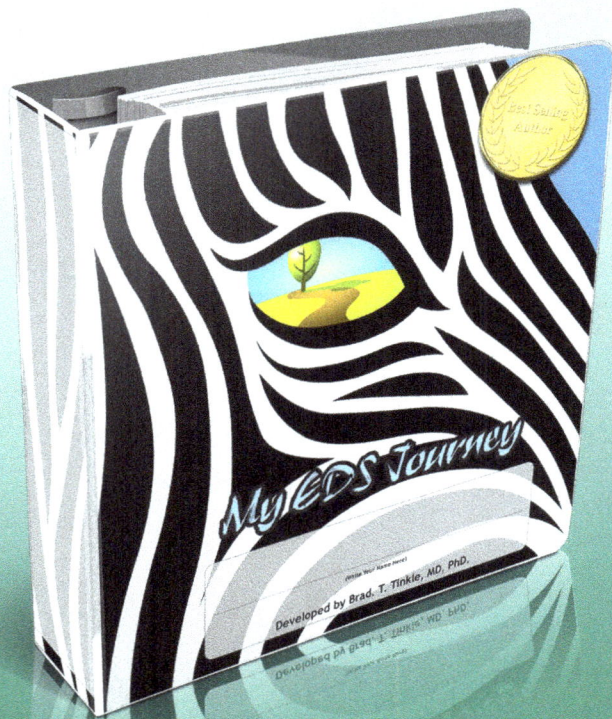

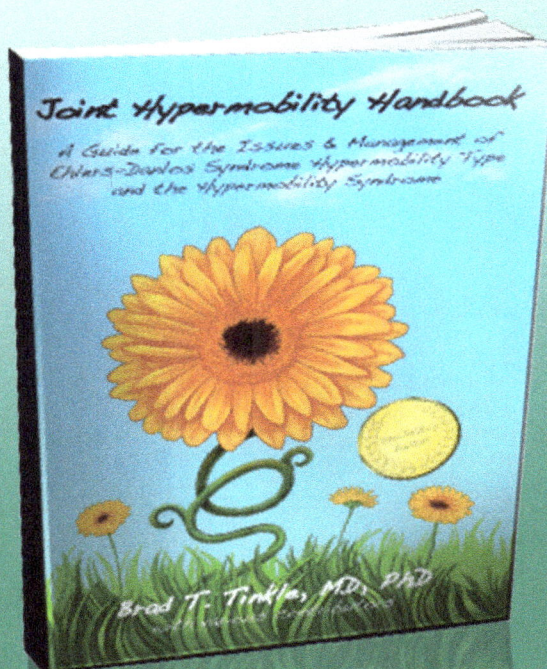

www.LeftPawPress.com

Featured In:

FOX BUSINESS abc NBC Los Angeles Times The Washington Post Pet Age Pet Product NEWS INTERNATIONAL.com Pet Business Pet World In

Become a PET FASHION PROFESSIONAL JUMPSTART MEMBER Completely FREE!

The JumpStart Membership swag bag includes:
advance notices on our exclusive events, weekly Pet Fashion Trend Updates, access to our Hangouts On Air, our Pet Fashion Professional Badge, AND our "Pet Biz Trade Show Marketing Secrets Unleashed" report!

- Pet Fashion Trends Updates Newsletter
- Pet Fashion Hangouts On Air
- Pet Fashion Professional Membership Badge
- Pet Biz Trade Show Marketing Secrets Unleashed eBook

GET YOUR SWAG BAG NOW!

International Association of PET FASHION PROFESSIONALS

WWW.PETFASHIONPROFESSIONALS.COM

Left Paw Press
is a **Proud Sponsor** of

Zachary Tinkle

2014 Central States Region Super Cups
ROOKIE OF THE YEAR

Rainbow Rocket paint scheme

53

TfR
Tinkle Family Racing

LEFT PAW Press

www.ZacharyTinkle.com

Get out of the Stands and into the FUN!

CSR Super Cups...
Where the Future of Racing Begins
www.SuperCupRacing.com

About the Author

Zachary Tinkle is a 12-year-old driving sensation based in Park Ridge, IL that currently races the #53 ½ size stock car minicup car (also known as super cups) and indoor electric go-karts.

He is the 2014 Central States Region (CSR) Rookie of the Year and placed Top 5 in championship points in his rookie season.

Tinkle has won a junior gas-powered indoor go-karting championship (Chicago Indoor Racing 2013) and three junior electric indoor go-karting championships (K1 Speed 2014 & 2015).

He has family ties to the Indianapolis and Richmond, IN areas and was born in Cincinnati, OH.

Zachary has aspirations of racing at the top levels of stock car racing including getting a ride with a NASCAR® team.

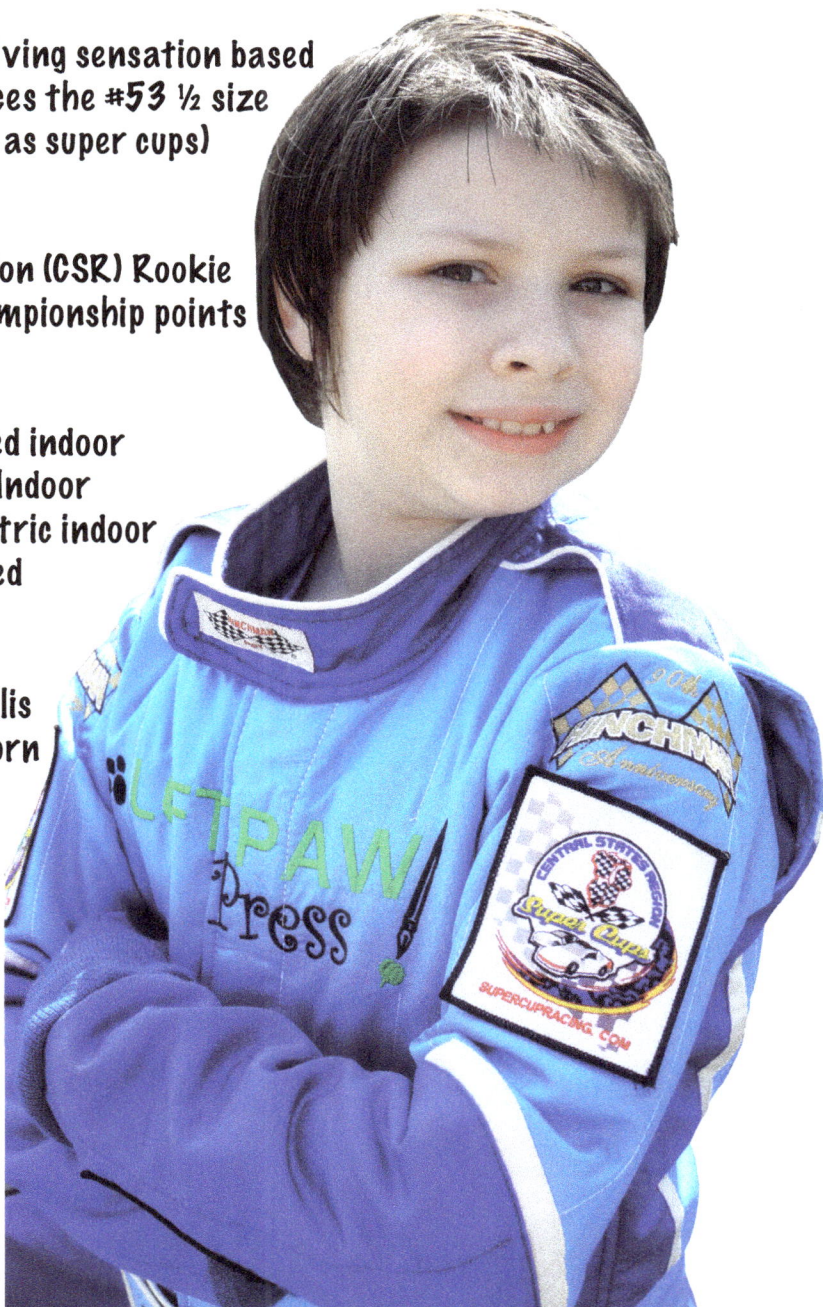

PUG CHILDREN'S FAIRY TALE SERIES
BOOKS ARE AVAILABLE IN COLOR
AND COLORING BOOK VERSIONS

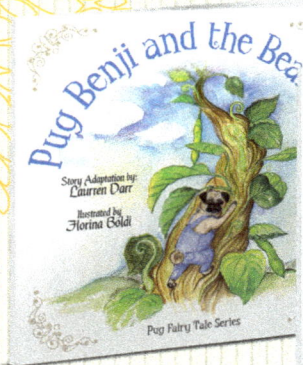

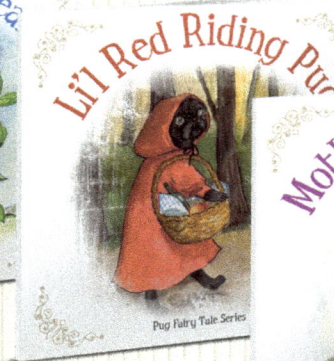

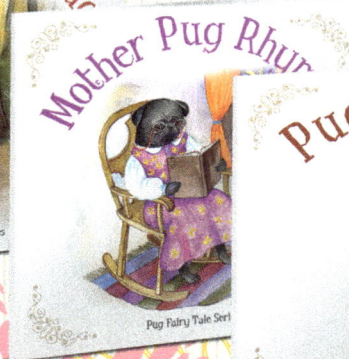

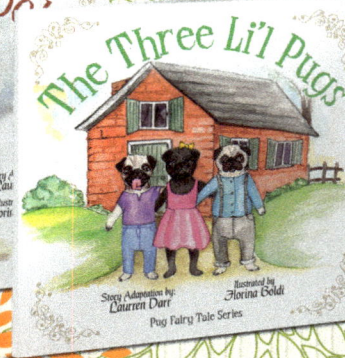

Pug Benji and the **Coloring Book**
Story Adaptation by: Laurren Darr
Illustrated by: Florina Boldi
Pug Fairy Tale Series

Li'l Red Riding **Coloring Book**
Story Adaptation by: Laurren Darr
Illustrated by: Florina Boldi

Mother Pug Rhym **Coloring Book**
Pug Fairy Tale Series

Pug in Boo **Coloring Book**
Pug Fairy Tale Series

The Three Li'l Pugs **Coloring Book**
Story Adaptation by: Laurren Darr
Illustrated by: Florina Boldi

Pug Benji and the Bea
Story Adaptation by: Laurren Darr
Illustrated by: Florina Boldi
Pug Fairy Tale Series

Li'l Red Riding Pug
Pug Fairy Tale Series

Mother Pug Rhym
Pug Fairy Tale Seri

Pug in Boo
Story A... Lau...
Illus... Floris...
Pug Fairy Tale Series

The Three Li'l Pugs
Story Adaptation by: Laurren Darr
Illustrated by: Florina Boldi
Pug Fairy Tale Series

LEFT PAW Press

www.LeftPawPress.com

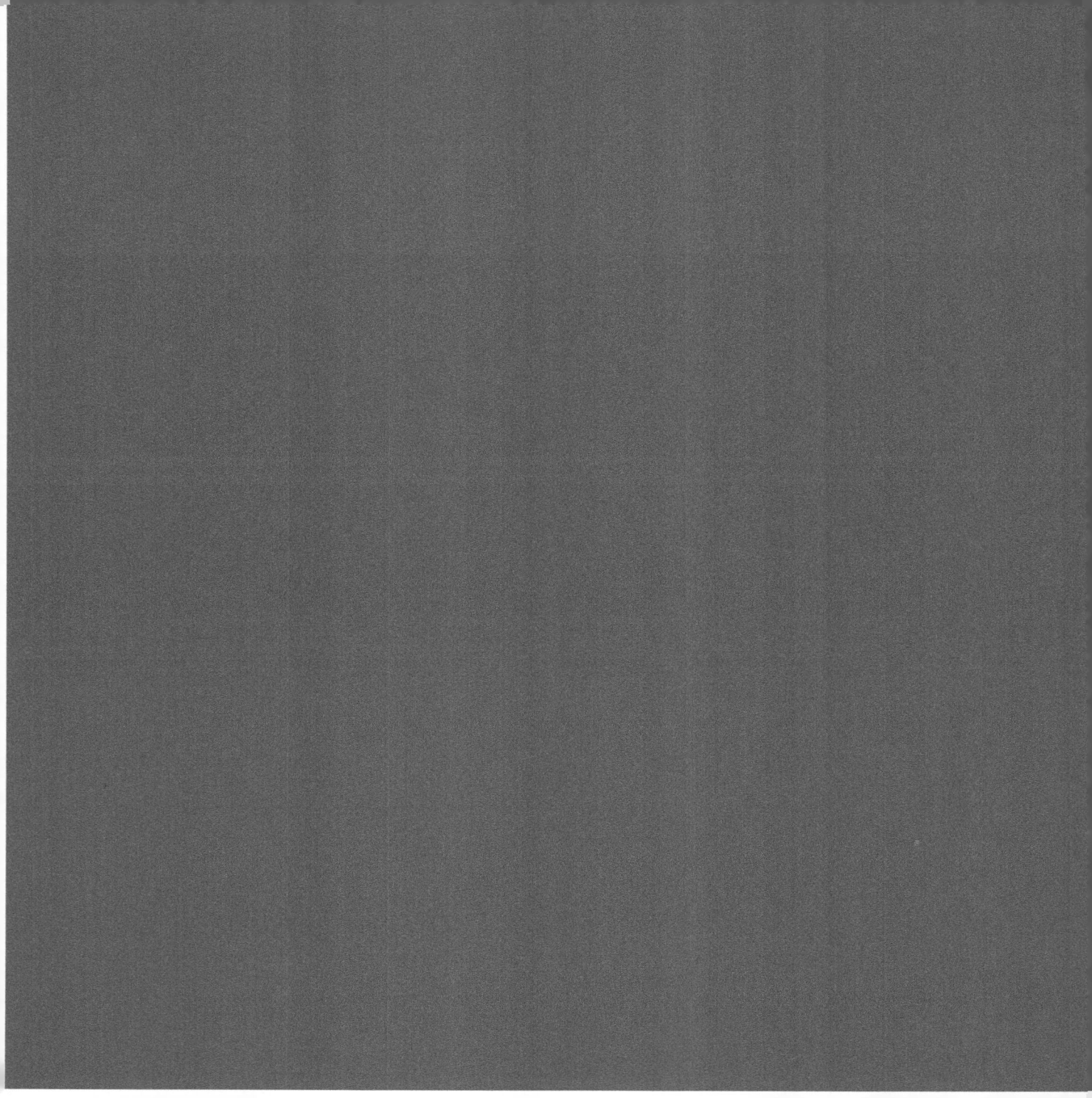

www.ingramcontent.com/pod-product-compliance
Lightning Source LLC
Chambersburg PA
CBHW061420090426
42744CB00018B/2077